This book is dedicated to the brave men and women of the United States military, both past and present, who have selflessly served our nation with honor, courage, and unwavering commitment.

# The Soldier's Prayer Book

Compiled by Carter Birmingham

# Prayer for Valor

Lord, You are my stronghold and my refuge; in the shadow of Your wings, I seek courage. As I stand in the face of adversity, whether on distant shores or at home, grant me the valor to act with bravery and honor. Infuse my heart with the strength of Your spirit, that I may face every challenge with unwavering courage and a steadfast faith.

Enable me, O God, to rise above fear and to uphold the values for which I stand. May my actions reflect Your glory, and may I serve as a beacon of hope and courage to my fellow soldiers and veterans. With Your guidance, Lord, I shall not falter but will carry forward the mission entrusted to me with boldness and integrity.

Amen.

# Prayer for Peaceful Rest

Heavenly Father, after the day's labors and the long stretches of vigilance, grant me the peaceful rest I seek. As I lay down my burdens, still my mind and ease the tensions of my heart. Wrap me in Your divine peace, that in my sleep, I may find the comfort and tranquility that eludes me in the wake of duty.

May Your presence be a soothing balm, restoring my spirit and renewing my strength. Protect me through the night, Lord, and let me rise refreshed, ready to continue serving with honor. In Your mercy, provide the same restful peace to my brothers and sisters in arms, that we all may know Your profound love even in our deepest slumber.

Amen.

# Prayer of Thanks for Safe Return

Lord Almighty, I lift my voice in profound gratitude for the safe return from duty. Your guiding hand has shielded me through dangers seen and unseen, and Your grace has brought me back to the warmth of home and family. Thank You for the embrace of loved ones, for the comfort of familiar sights, and for the peace that settles in my heart knowing I am home.

As I rejoice in this reunion, I also remember my fellow soldiers still in the field. Extend to them Your protection and lead them safely home. Help me to cherish each moment of peace and to use this gift of safety to strengthen the bonds with those I love. With a thankful heart, I acknowledge Your mercy and love that sustain me always.

Amen.

# Prayer for Fallen Comrades

Lord God, I hold in my heart the memory of my fallen comrades, those who have laid down their lives in service. In this solemn moment, I honor their sacrifice and cherish the valor and dedication with which they served. May their spirits find peace in Your eternal embrace, and may their families find solace in their brave legacy.

Grant us, who continue in their absence, the strength to carry forward the torch of freedom and justice they upheld. Let us live in a manner worthy of their sacrifice, remembering always the cost at which our peace is bought. Bless us with the courage to face each day with honor, as we strive to ensure their sacrifice was not in vain.

Amen.

# Prayer for Leadership

Heavenly Father, I pray for wisdom and discernment for our military leaders, that they may navigate the complexities of their responsibilities with clarity and ethical conviction. Bestow upon them the courage to make decisions that safeguard the well-being of those under their command and the integrity of our nation. Guide their hearts and minds in justice, humility, and the pursuit of peace.

Empower them, Lord, with the foresight to see beyond the immediate, understanding the long-term impacts of their choices. Strengthen their resolve to act honorably and justly in all circumstances, fostering a culture of respect, unity, and dedication among those they lead. May their leadership reflect Your divine guidance, promoting a legacy of service and honor for generations to come.

Amen.

# Prayer for Protection

Heavenly Father, in times of danger and uncertainty, I seek Your protective embrace. Surround me and my fellow service members with Your mighty presence; shield us from harm and guide us through every challenge. Let Your wisdom be our path, and Your strength our shield, as we navigate the perils that lie before us.

Instill in us a spirit of courage and vigilance, that we may uphold our duties without fear. Watch over us, O Lord, and extend Your hand of safety to our families who wait with hopeful hearts for our safe return. May we trust in Your divine protection and feel the reassurance of Your unfailing love in every moment of risk.

Amen.

# Prayer for Unity

Father in Heaven, bind us together with the strong cords of brotherhood and sisterhood as we serve side by side in the defense of our nation. Let unity prevail among us, breaking down barriers of division and building bridges of mutual respect and understanding. In our shared mission, inspire us to look beyond individual differences and towards our common goals.

Nurture in our hearts a deep sense of camaraderie, that we may support one another in every challenge and rejoice together in every victory. May our bonds of fellowship be strengthened by Your love, guiding us to act as one body, moved by one spirit, dedicated to the peace and security of our beloved country.

Amen.

# Prayer for the Families

Lord, I lift up the families of those who serve in our military, asking for Your strength and support to fill their homes. During times of separation and uncertainty, be their steadfast comfort and unshakable foundation. Bless them with resilience as they manage daily life with the weight of worry, and fill their hearts with peace, knowing their loved ones are under Your watchful care.

Provide these families with a strong community that understands and shares their struggles and triumphs. Encourage them through friendships and networks that offer practical support and emotional solidarity. May they sense Your presence in every moment of need, finding solace in Your promises and courage in Your faithfulness.

Amen.

# Prayer for Wisdom

Gracious God, grant me the gift of wisdom that I may discern the best paths in the complex situations I face. Illuminate my mind with Your light so that I may see clearly, understand deeply, and act wisely. Help me to weigh decisions with prudence and to lead with foresight, reflecting Your divine guidance in all my actions.

In moments of uncertainty, provide me with the clarity I need to navigate challenges with confidence and integrity. Let Your wisdom guide me, not only in achieving immediate goals but also in contributing to the greater good. Strengthen my resolve to serve honorably, making choices that honor You and advance the cause of justice and peace.

Amen.

# Prayer for Hope

Lord, in these challenging times, I turn to You seeking hope to uplift my spirit. Let Your light pierce through the shadows of despair and doubt that may cloud my path. Rekindle in my heart the flame of hope that guides me through uncertainty and fortifies me against fear. May Your promises and Your steadfast love serve as anchors, keeping my hope alive and vibrant even in the darkest moments.

Encourage me, Father, and use me as a vessel to bring hope to others within my reach. Grant that through my words and actions, those around me might also feel the surge of hope that comes from You. May this hope not only sustain us but propel us forward to face the challenges ahead with courage and joy.

Amen.

# Prayer for Forgiveness

Heavenly Father, I come before You seeking forgiveness for the times I have fallen short of Your glory, both in action and in thought. In the midst of duty and the pressures it brings, I have at times lost my way, reacting in ways that do not reflect Your love and mercy. Wash me clean with Your grace, and renew a right spirit within me, that I may live in the light of Your forgiveness.

Guide me in the paths of reconciliation, that I may extend pardon to others as freely as You have granted it to me. Help me to mend bridges that have been damaged and to restore relationships that have been strained. In Your mercy, teach me to forgive myself and to move forward with the peace and assurance that comes from Your absolution.

Amen.

# Prayer for Resilience

Lord, as I face trials that test my strength and resolve, I seek Your support to build my resilience. Fortify my spirit with Your enduring power, so that I may not waver under the weight of challenges but rise stronger with each step forward. Help me to persevere, steadfast in the knowledge that You are with me, molding my character and preparing me for the path ahead.

Inspire in me a heart of courage and a spirit of endurance, that I may embrace each trial as an opportunity for growth and deeper reliance on You. May I find in Your presence the comfort and motivation to continue, no matter the obstacles, and may my resilience be a testament to Your sustaining grace.

Amen.

# Prayer for Our Nation

Almighty God, I lift up our nation before You, seeking Your blessings and prosperity for the United States of America. Guide our leaders with Your wisdom, protect our people with Your strength, and enrich our land with Your abundance. May Your hand be upon this nation, fostering unity, peace, and justice across our states, so that we might thrive under Your grace and continue to be a beacon of hope and freedom to the world.

Bless our communities with harmony and our endeavors with success, ensuring that every corner of our great nation prospers. Instill in us a spirit of cooperation and respect, that together we may overcome challenges and build a future that honors Your name. May we always remember our dependence on You, and may our gratitude for Your countless blessings be reflected in how we steward the liberty and wealth You have bestowed upon us.

Amen.

# Prayer for Freedom

Heavenly Father, I thank You for the precious gift of freedom, a blessing that we cherish deeply in our hearts. As a nation and as individuals, help us to not take for granted the liberty we enjoy. Instill in us a relentless spirit to preserve and protect this freedom, ensuring it remains intact for future generations. Let us be vigilant stewards of the liberty You have granted, using it to promote justice, peace, and dignity for all.

Guide us, Lord, in the paths of responsibility and righteousness, so that our actions may reflect the values upon which our freedom was founded. Strengthen our resolve to stand against any forces that threaten to diminish our rights or the rights of others. May our appreciation for our freedom manifest in our respect for each other, uniting us under Your divine providence.

Amen.

# Prayer for the Lonely

Father in Heaven, in moments of solitude and separation from those I love, I seek Your comforting presence. Fill the spaces of loneliness with Your love, and guide me towards the companionship and community I long for. Open my heart to new relationships that bring mutual encouragement and understanding, and help me to be a friend to others as I seek friendship for myself.

Bless me, Lord, with a sense of belonging wherever I am—whether on duty or at home. Connect me with people who share a kindred spirit, creating bonds that reflect Your love and fellowship. In my times of isolation, remind me that You are always with me, and that in Your vast family, I am never truly alone.

Amen.

# Prayer for the Anxious

Lord, in moments when anxiety grips my heart and clouds my mind, I come to You seeking peace. Calm the storm of my worries and replace my fears with Your profound tranquility. Help me to rest in the assurance of Your protective embrace, trusting that You are in control and that You provide for all my needs according to Your perfect plan.

Teach me, Father, to breathe deeply of Your peace in every anxious moment. May Your presence envelop me like a gentle breeze, refreshing my spirit and quieting my thoughts. Grant me the strength to face each day with confidence, not in my own abilities, but in Your ceaseless love and care for me.

Amen.

# Prayer for Patience

Gracious God, in the rush of duties and the pressure of deadlines, grant me the virtue of patience. Help me to endure discomfort without complaint and to accept delays with composure. Teach me to tolerate imperfections in myself and in others, offering grace as generously as You have given it to me. Let patience refine my character and enhance my leadership, making me a model of calm in the midst of storms.

Instruct my heart to wait peacefully for outcomes and to trust in Your timing for all things. As I serve, let me not rush to judgment or action, but consider all paths with wisdom and patience. Through challenges, may I grow stronger and more patient, embodying the steadfastness that You show in all Your works.

Amen.

# Prayer for Humility

Lord, as I fulfill my duties, imbue me with the grace of humility. Let me serve not for recognition or reward, but out of a genuine desire to do Your will and to aid my fellow humans. Help me to remember that true strength lies in humility, and that leadership is rooted in serving others. Keep my heart from pride and my mind from arrogance, that I may always remember my dependence on You and on those around me.

Guide me to value the contributions of others, acknowledging that every role is critical to our shared success and that no task is insignificant. Teach me to uplift others as I strive to fulfill my responsibilities, always seeking to place the welfare of others above my own. In this way, may my life reflect the humility of Christ, who came not to be served, but to serve.

Amen.

# Prayer for Strength

Heavenly Father, grant me the strength both in body and spirit to face the tasks and trials that come my way. Bolster my physical endurance to withstand the rigors demanded by my duties, and fortify my soul with the courage and resilience needed to persevere through challenges. Let Your mighty power flow through me, so that I may stand firm against adversity and continue my service with vigor and vitality.

Nurture within me a spirit of steadfastness, that I may not falter nor grow weary in my journey. As I draw upon Your endless strength, renew my hope and refresh my spirit daily, so that I may reflect Your grace and power in all my actions and decisions. Through Your sustaining love, I am made strong and ready to fulfill my calling with honor and commitment.

Amen.

# Prayer for the Deployed

Father in Heaven, as I serve far from home, surround me with Your protection and keep me safe in the shadow of Your wings. Watch over me in every operation, every mission, and in the quiet moments in between. Strengthen my faith while I am deployed, that I may carry the assurance of Your presence wherever I am called to go. Grant me the courage to face each day, knowing You are with me, guiding and guarding my every step.

Uphold my family and loved ones back home with Your comforting hand, filling their hearts with peace and their lives with joy despite our separation. May they feel connected to me through the bond of Your love, which transcends all distances. Keep us steadfast in our faith and hopeful for the day of joyful reunion.

Amen.

# Prayer for Veterans

Lord, I lift up my fellow veterans who have served alongside me and before me, asking for Your blessings upon each of their lives. Recognize their sacrifices, great and small, and fill their days with Your peace and fulfillment. Help our nation to honor and care for them, providing the support and recognition they deserve. May their contributions never be forgotten, and may they find joy and pride in their service to our country.

Grant wisdom to those who provide care and make decisions that affect veterans' lives, that they may do so with compassion and justice. Ease the burdens carried by those who bear the scars of service, both visible and unseen. Strengthen our community's commitment to uplifting those who have given so much, ensuring that they receive the respect, healthcare, and opportunities they rightly earned.

Amen.

# Prayer for Healing

Lord, I seek Your healing touch upon my life and the lives of my comrades, as we carry both visible and hidden wounds from our service. Pour out Your grace to mend broken bodies, soothe tormented minds, and heal aching hearts. Let Your healing be a beacon of hope in our lives, reminding us that no injury is too deep for Your loving hand to repair. Rejuvenate our spirits, that we may find new strength and joy in each day under Your watchful care.

Surround us with a community of support, understanding, and love—people who can walk alongside us in our journey towards recovery. Provide us with the resources and care we need, and guide those who tend to our wounds with skill and compassion. Through Your power, may we rise each day with renewed purpose and peace, confident in Your promises of restoration and new beginnings.

Amen.

# Prayer for Guidance

Heavenly Father, as I navigate both my personal and military life, I earnestly seek Your guidance to light my path. In decisions large and small, let Your wisdom prevail over my own understanding. Help me to discern Your will, to recognize the right choices that lead to peace and growth. Strengthen my resolve to follow Your lead, trusting that You know what is best for me and those I am called to serve.

Provide clarity amid confusion and insight in complexity, that I may act with confidence knowing I am aligned with Your purposes. May Your guiding hand be evident in my relationships, my career, and every aspect of my life. Let me be a reflection of Your love and wisdom as I lead, serve, and grow in the roles You have entrusted to me.

Amen.

# Prayer for Military Spouses

Lord, I lift up the spouses of those who serve in our military, recognizing the unique challenges and sacrifices they face each day. Strengthen their hearts with Your love and resilience as they manage the home front, often under the weight of uncertainty and long separations. Grant them peace and patience, and the wisdom to navigate the complexities of military life with grace and courage.

Bless these dedicated partners with a supportive community that understands their struggles and shares their burdens. Provide them with resources that ease their responsibilities and offer comfort in times of stress. May they feel Your presence as a constant source of strength and assurance, knowing that they are not alone in their journey.

Amen.

# Prayer for Trust

Heavenly Father, instill in me a spirit of trust towards those who lead and those who stand beside me. In times of doubt and uncertainty, help me to see the integrity and good intentions of my leaders and peers. Strengthen our bonds, that together we might build a foundation of mutual respect and confidence, essential for overcoming the challenges we face as a team.

Guide our leaders to be examples of transparency and honesty, fostering an environment where trust thrives and where every team member feels valued and understood. Allow my interactions to reflect a trust that is rooted in Your love and wisdom, encouraging others to act similarly. May this trust lead us to greater unity and effectiveness in all our endeavors.

Amen.

# Prayer for Integrity

Lord Almighty, I ask for Your guidance to uphold integrity in every aspect of my life. As I serve, whether in uniform or in civilian roles, imbue me with the courage to act honestly and uphold high moral standards. Let my actions reflect the righteousness of Your teachings, and help me to remain true to my values even when faced with difficult choices or when no one is watching.

Strengthen my resolve to conduct myself with honor and dignity, ensuring that my words align with my deeds. May I be a beacon of integrity for my colleagues and those I lead, inspiring them to embrace honesty as the cornerstone of their own actions. Through Your divine assistance, may we collectively foster an environment of trust and ethical behavior that glorifies Your name.

Amen.

# Prayer for Thanksgiving

Gracious God, I come before You with a heart overflowing with gratitude for the many blessings You have bestowed upon me. In moments of joy and in times of trial, Your steadfast love remains a source of comfort and strength. Thank you for the protection, provision, and peace that You continuously offer, and for the unwavering support of family, friends, and fellow service members.

As I reflect on these gifts, help me to always acknowledge Your hand in all things. May my life be a testament to Your generosity, and may I share the abundance of Your blessings with others. Teach me to remain thankful in all circumstances, recognizing every good thing comes from You, and using my gratitude to uplift and inspire those around me.

Amen.

# Prayer for Reflection

Heavenly Father, grant me moments of quiet reflection amidst the busyness and demands of my duties. In these times of solitude, help me to ponder the depth of Your love and the breadth of Your wisdom. Let these moments of contemplation enrich my understanding of Your ways and deepen my appreciation for the life You have given me. Show me the lessons You have for me in each experience, and help me to grow in spiritual maturity and understanding.

As I reflect, bring clarity to my thoughts and decisions, revealing paths that align with Your will. May this introspective practice strengthen my connection with You and illuminate my journey, guiding my steps in truth and righteousness. Through reflection, may I become more attuned to Your voice and more aware of the needs of those around me, serving as a better instrument of Your peace.

Amen.

# Prayer for New Recruits

Lord, I lift up the new recruits who have stepped forward to serve. As they begin their journey in the military, grant them courage to face the challenges ahead and the adaptability to thrive in their new roles. Fill their hearts with determination and strength, that they may embrace each task with confidence and a willingness to learn. Protect them, Father, as they adapt to the demands of military life, and inspire them with a clear sense of purpose and commitment.

Help these young men and women to quickly find their footing, integrating smoothly with their units and forming bonds that will support them through trials and triumphs. Equip them with the resilience needed to overcome obstacles and the flexibility to navigate the ever-changing landscapes of their service. May they grow not only in skill but also in character, becoming strong leaders and dedicated defenders of our nation.

Amen.

# Prayer for Retirement

Heavenly Father, as I approach the threshold of retirement from military service, guide me through this significant transition. Open new doors of opportunity where I can continue to use my skills and experiences in meaningful ways. Fill my heart with enthusiasm for the new chapters ahead, and help me to embrace change with an open mind and a willing spirit.

Bless this new beginning with Your presence and peace, ensuring that I carry forward the lessons and friendships I have gained over the years. Provide me with clarity as I explore new pursuits and build a life outside the uniform. May this next phase of my journey be rich with purpose and joy, marked by Your love and guided by Your wisdom.

Amen.

# Prayer for Reconciliation

Father in Heaven, I pray for reconciliation where there is discord, seeking Your divine intervention to mend what has been broken and soothe what has been stirred. Guide us toward mutual understanding and peace, smoothing the rough edges of our interactions and healing the divisions that may exist. Instill in us the grace to listen with open hearts, to speak with gentle honesty, and to forgive with the breadth of Your mercy.

Help us, Lord, to see one another through Your eyes—valuing each person's dignity and worth. Where misunderstandings have caused rifts, provide us the humility and strength to bridge gaps and foster unity. May our efforts at reconciliation reflect Your love, promoting harmony and cooperation, and may our relationships be restored to reflect the unity You desire for all Your children.

Amen.

# Prayer for Justice

Lord God, You are the foundation of justice and righteousness. I pray that Your principles of fairness and equity may permeate our actions and decisions, both in the military and in our broader community. Inspire our leaders and all who wield authority to act justly, to love mercy, and to walk humbly with You. May we uphold the highest standards of integrity and fairness, ensuring that no one is denied the rights and respect they deserve.

Strengthen us to be advocates for justice, to stand firm against inequality, and to protect the vulnerable. Help us to recognize our own biases and to act to correct them, striving always for a world that reflects Your divine order. In our quest for justice, let us be guided by Your wisdom and fortified by Your strength, so that in all things, Your will may be done on earth as it is in heaven.

Amen.

# Prayer for Military Chaplains

Heavenly Father, I lift up the military chaplains who serve as spiritual guides and counselors among us. Grant them an abundance of Your wisdom and compassion as they minister to the diverse needs of those in service. Strengthen their resolve and deepen their understanding, that they might provide comfort and guidance with sensitivity and grace. Equip them with Your peace and the right words in times of crisis, enabling them to be beacons of hope and sources of light in the darkest moments.

Bless their ministry, Lord, that through their work, many may come to know Your love more deeply. Protect them in their travels and their toil, and replenish their spirits when they are weary. May their presence bring unity and spiritual growth within the ranks, and may they themselves feel the support and prayerful backing of the community they serve.

Amen.

# Prayer for National Leaders

Lord Almighty, I pray for our national leaders, who carry the heavy responsibility of guiding our country through times of peace and crisis. Grant them wisdom beyond their own understanding and counsel that aligns with Your will. May they seek Your guidance diligently as they make decisions that affect the lives of countless people and shape the future of our nation. Instill in them a spirit of righteousness, that their governance may be just, and their actions may promote the welfare and prosperity of all citizens.

Help them to lead with integrity and courage, setting aside personal gains for the greater good. Encourage them to listen with empathy to the diverse voices of our people, responding with policies that uphold dignity and justice for every individual. May their leadership bring honor to our nation and reflect Your divine principles, leading us toward a more united and prosperous society.

Amen.

# Prayer for International Peace

Heavenly Father, I come before You to pray for peace across our world. Amidst global tensions and conflicts, I ask for Your divine intervention to sow seeds of harmony and cooperation among nations. Guide the hearts and minds of world leaders towards collaboration rather than confrontation, seeking resolutions that benefit all of humanity. Help us to transcend boundaries and differences, fostering a global community united in purpose and mutual respect.

Inspire us, Lord, to work tirelessly for peace, to be advocates for justice, and to be agents of reconciliation in our interactions both near and far. May our efforts reflect Your call for love and unity, and may we see the fruits of these labors as nations come together to solve common problems and celebrate shared successes. Let us not lose hope in the pursuit of a more peaceful world, trusting in Your power to transform and heal.

Amen.

# Prayer for Daily Duties

Father, as I face my daily duties, grant me the dedication to perform each task with excellence and integrity. In the routine responsibilities that shape my days, infuse me with a sense of purpose and a commitment to serve as though I am serving You. Help me to see the value in the smallest tasks and to understand how even these contribute to the greater mission. Strengthen my resolve to approach each day with energy and enthusiasm, honoring You through my work.

Keep my spirit uplifted when the routine becomes mundane, and remind me of the importance of discipline and diligence. May my actions inspire others to commit fully to their responsibilities, creating a culture of accountability and excellence. In all things, let me be a testament to Your grace, working wholeheartedly and giving my best.

Amen.

# Prayer for Moral Courage

Lord, in moments when fear and doubt cloud my judgment, I pray for the moral courage to choose the right action. Strengthen my heart to stand firm in my values, even when it's difficult or when I stand alone. Infuse my spirit with the courage that comes from knowing You are with me, guiding me to act justly and honorably in every circumstance. Help me to embody the integrity and bravery that define true leadership and moral fortitude.

Illuminate the path of righteousness for me, and provide the resolve to follow it, regardless of the personal cost. May I be an example to those around me by showing what it means to act courageously and ethically, inspired by Your divine example. Let my actions reflect Your love and commitment to justice, and may I find strength in Your presence as I face the challenges ahead.

Amen.

# Prayer for Sacrifice

Heavenly Father, I am called to a life of sacrifice, following the example of Christ who gave Himself for all. Help me to embrace this call willingly and selflessly, finding honor in the act of giving for the benefit of others. Instill in me a generous spirit that seeks not my own comfort, but the welfare and safety of those I serve alongside and those we aim to protect. Let my actions reflect the depth of my commitment and the sincerity of my sacrifice.

May this path of sacrifice bring me closer to You, Lord, and may it be a testament to my devotion and love for my fellow humans. Grant me the strength to persevere when the cost is high, and the grace to act with kindness and courage, knowing that my sacrifices have a purpose in Your greater plan. Bless my efforts, and let them contribute to peace and justice in the world.

Amen.

# Prayer for the Seas

Lord, who calmed the storm and walked upon the waters, I ask Your blessings upon the Navy, those who traverse the vast oceans to protect and serve. Guide them safely through both calm and turbulent seas. Grant them wisdom and vigilance in their duties, that they may operate their vessels with skill and honor. Protect them from the perils of the deep and keep their paths clear of adversaries and natural threats.

Provide comfort to their families who wait at home, granting them peace of mind and steadfast hope. May the sailors feel Your presence aboard every ship and submarine, knowing they are never beyond Your watchful eyes. Strengthen their resolve and unity as they serve on the seas, and may their efforts contribute to peace and security across the globe.

Amen.

# Prayer for the Skies

Lord Almighty, Creator of the heavens and the earth, I lift up the brave men and women of the Air Force as they soar through the skies in their mission to protect and defend. Surround them with Your protection as they navigate the vast expanses above us, ensuring their safe passage through both clear and troubled skies. Grant them precision and clarity in their tasks, that they may fulfill their duties with excellence and integrity.

Bless the pilots, crew, and support teams with your wisdom and strength. May they find reassurance in Your omnipresent care, knowing that they are guided by Your hand. Keep their aircraft safe, their missions successful, and their spirits high. Let them serve as guardians of peace in the air, as they rely on Your divine guidance and protection.

Amen.

# Prayer for the Land

Heavenly Father, I call upon Your strength and support for the Army, those who serve diligently on the land, guarding our freedoms and upholding justice. Endow them with courage and resilience as they face the myriad challenges of their duties, from the quiet of peacetime to the trials of conflict. Strengthen their resolve and fortify their spirits, that they may stand firm in the face of adversity, embodying the virtues of honor and duty.

Bless each soldier with robust health and unwavering determination. May their efforts be underpinned by Your wisdom and guided by Your hand. Protect them in every deployment and operation, and may their endeavors on the land contribute to a safer, more peaceful world. Let their service be a testament to their dedication to our nation and their commitment to Your divine principles of righteousness and peace.

Amen.

# Prayer for the Homefront

Lord, I pray for the homefront, the foundation from which we venture and to which we return. Guard our homes and communities with Your peace and provide security as we support those who serve far from our shores. Instill in us a spirit of unity and support, that we might create a sanctuary of warmth and safety for our families and neighbors. Help us to nurture an environment where love and harmony flourish, protecting us from the fears and disruptions of the world.

Bless the efforts of all who contribute to maintaining peace and stability in our nation. Grant wisdom to our leaders and officials, that they may make decisions that safeguard our liberties and promote the common good. May our communities reflect the strength and serenity of Your kingdom, and may we always find rest and reassurance at home, knowing it is under Your watchful care.

Amen.

# Prayer for the Future

Heavenly Father, as I look toward the future, I place my hopes and dreams in Your hands, trusting in Your divine guidance to lead the way. Illuminate the path ahead with Your wisdom, enabling me to move forward with confidence and clarity. Grant me the vision to see beyond the immediate, to the possibilities that You have in store for me, my fellow service members, and our nation. Inspire us all with a renewed sense of purpose and a steadfast commitment to our calling, that we may continue to serve honorably and effectively.

Encourage us, Lord, to embrace the challenges and changes that come with time, using them as opportunities for growth and advancement. May our future endeavors be marked by innovation and integrity, reflecting Your love and justice in every action. Help us to build a legacy that honors You and benefits those who will follow in our footsteps, securing a future filled with peace, prosperity, and Your everlasting grace.

Amen.

# Prayer for Persistence

Lord, grant me the strength to persist through the trials and tribulations that test my resolve. In the face of adversity, whether in the calm of routine or the chaos of conflict, fortify my spirit to continue undeterred. Help me to draw upon Your endless reserves of grace and perseverance, standing steadfast in my commitments and duties. Let not the weight of challenges deter me, but rather, let them be opportunities to demonstrate my dedication and resilience.

Renew my energy each day, Lord, and instill in me a relentless spirit that is unyielding in the pursuit of excellence and service. May I find encouragement in Your promises, knowing that You are with me, guiding and supporting my efforts. In my weakest moments, remind me of the strength that comes from You, and inspire me to push forward with courage and unflagging zeal.

Amen.

# Prayer for Memorial Day

Heavenly Father, as we observe Memorial Day, we pause to honor the valiant men and women who have served our nation with extraordinary courage and dedication. We remember those who laid down their lives for the freedoms we cherish, asking You to bless their memories and comfort their families. Help us to never forget the sacrifices made on our behalf, that their legacy may continue to inspire generations and their valor be eternally engraved in our national consciousness.

May this day of remembrance deepen our gratitude for the peace and liberty we enjoy, and renew our commitment to uphold the ideals for which they fought. Stir in our hearts a profound respect for our military history and a heartfelt appreciation for the immense cost of our freedom. Let us honor them not just with words, but through our actions and lives that strive for peace and justice under Your divine guidance.

Amen.

# Prayer for Spiritual Armor

Lord, as I face the challenges and trials both seen and unseen, I ask for Your spiritual armor to protect me. Clothe me in Your helmet of salvation, breastplate of righteousness, belt of truth, shield of faith, shoes of peace, and the sword of the Spirit, which is Your Word. Let these pieces shield my spirit from the snares and temptations of the enemy, fortifying my heart and mind in Christ Jesus.

Strengthen me with Your might and power, that I may stand firm against all spiritual forces of evil. Guide my thoughts and actions, so that I may walk in Your ways and resist the deceptions that seek to lead me astray. As I serve in my capacity, let me be a beacon of Your light, protected by Your grace and committed to the path of righteousness.

Amen.

# Prayer for Compassion

Heavenly Father, I pray that You cultivate in me a heart of compassion, rich in kindness and empathy. As I interact with others, whether they be comrades, family, or strangers, imbue my words and actions with gentleness and understanding. Help me to see beyond the surface, recognizing the struggles and needs that lie within those I meet. May Your love guide my behavior, making me an instrument of Your grace in every encounter.

Encourage me, Lord, to act with patience and warmth, offering support where it is needed and a listening ear where it is sought. In conflicts, grant me the ability to respond with a spirit of reconciliation and peace, fostering an environment where compassion prevails over discord. Through my example, may others be inspired to embrace kindness as a way of life, creating ripples of goodwill wherever we go.

Amen.

# Prayer for Discipline

Lord, grant me the discipline to govern my actions and emotions, fostering self-control that anchors me in all aspects of life. In the face of temptations or challenges, provide me with the strength to choose the path that honors You and upholds my duties. Help me to maintain order in my personal and professional life, ensuring that I act not out of impulse but with thoughtful consideration and respect for the consequences of my actions.

Empower me to be a model of discipline for those around me, showing the benefits of a well-ordered life. May Your wisdom guide my decisions, and may Your spirit strengthen my resolve to practice restraint and diligence. Let discipline be not only a personal virtue but a cornerstone of my interactions and responsibilities, enhancing my effectiveness and integrity as I serve.

Amen.

# Prayer for Wisdom in Conflict

Heavenly Father, in moments of conflict and disagreement, I seek Your wisdom to navigate through discord with grace and insight. Help me to understand not only the surface tensions but the deeper issues at play. Equip me with the discernment to respond thoughtfully and effectively, aiming for resolutions that heal rather than harm. May my words bring clarity and foster understanding, bridging divides with the guidance of Your Holy Spirit.

Instill in me a calm spirit and a keen mind in the midst of disputes, that I may act as a peacemaker who reflects Your love and justice. Let me be an instrument of Your peace, using wisdom to turn contention into opportunities for growth and reconciliation. Through these challenges, mold my character and strengthen my leadership, making me a testament to Your transformative power in all situations.

Amen.

# Prayer for a Clear Mind

Lord, I come before You seeking clarity of mind amidst the complexities and pressures of my duties. Clear away any confusion and doubt that may cloud my judgment, enabling me to think sharply and act wisely. Illuminate my path with Your light, so that I may see each situation with discernment and respond with precision. Help me to focus on the tasks at hand with full attention, guided by Your wisdom in every decision I make.

Empower me, Father, to organize my thoughts and prioritize my actions according to Your will. Let peace reign in my mind, replacing turmoil with tranquility and uncertainty with understanding. As I navigate through the challenges of my service, maintain my thoughts aligned with Your purpose, ensuring that my actions follow suit, leading to outcomes that glorify You and benefit those I am called to serve.

Amen.

# Prayer for Mission Success

Lord Almighty, as I embark on missions and face challenges, guide me towards success in achieving the objectives set before me. Strengthen my resolve and sharpen my skills, that I may navigate each task with precision and effectiveness. Surround me with Your favor and wisdom, enabling me and my team to overcome obstacles and deliver results that contribute to our collective goals.

Bless our efforts with unity and cooperation, ensuring that each member contributes their best under Your watchful eye. Let us find innovative solutions and maintain steadfast dedication to our mission, driven by a desire to serve well and honorably. May our work not only meet the immediate aims but also pave the way for lasting peace and stability, reflecting Your glory and upholding our commitment to excellence.

Amen.

# Prayer for the Injured

Heavenly Father, I come before You with a heart full of concern for my fellow service members who are injured, asking for Your healing touch upon their lives. Speed their recovery, Lord, and restore them to full health. Mend their wounds, soothe their pain, and heal their scars, both visible and invisible. Provide them with the medical care and support they need to make a complete recovery, and fill their spirits with hope and perseverance during this challenging time.

Surround them with love and compassion, ensuring that they are never alone in their journey to healing. Strengthen their bodies and minds each day, and inspire those around them to offer assistance and encouragement. May their healing process be a testament to Your miraculous power and Your unending love for Your children.

Amen.

# Prayer for Calmness

Father, in the midst of the chaos and turbulence that often surround me, I seek the serenity that only You can provide. Calm my mind and steady my heart as I navigate through the storms of life. Help me to remain composed under pressure, reflecting Your peace in every action and decision. Let Your tranquility envelop me, shielding me from anxiety and stress, and instilling in me a profound sense of calm that surpasses all understanding.

Grant me the grace to spread this peace to others who may also feel overwhelmed by the chaos around them. Teach me to be a source of stability, a calming presence in turbulent times. May my words and deeds bring reassurance and hope, drawing on Your endless well of peace to sustain not only myself but also those I interact with.

Amen.

# Prayer for Prisoners of War

Heavenly Father, I lift up the prisoners of war and those missing in action, held away from their homes and loved ones. In their isolation and hardship, be their comfort, their strength, and their hope. Protect them from despair, sustain their spirits, and keep alive their hope for a safe return. May Your presence be felt profoundly in their hearts, reminding them that they are never forgotten, neither by You nor by those who await their return.

I pray earnestly for the swift and safe return of all who are held captive. Work within the hearts and minds of those who hold them, leading to a resolution that brings them home. Strengthen their families, who endure the pain of separation and the torment of uncertainty. May they find peace in Your assurances and perseverance in their advocacy for their loved ones' return. Lord, hear our prayers and reunite these brave souls with their families.

Amen.

# Prayer for Military Nurses and Doctors

Lord, I lift up the dedicated military nurses and doctors who serve with commitment and compassion. Bless their hands and hearts as they provide care to those in need. Grant them exceptional skill and deep wisdom in their medical duties, that through their efforts, health may be restored and lives saved. Infuse their work with Your grace, enabling them to heal not only physical wounds but also to soothe troubled spirits.

Strengthen them in their challenging work, especially when they face overwhelming cases or when fatigue sets in. Renew their energy and sustain their passion for helping others. May they always find in their profession a profound sense of calling and fulfillment, knowing that their care extends Your love and mercy. Keep them safe and healthy as they tend to others, and let their service be a beacon of hope and healing within the military community.

Amen.

# Prayer for Truth

Father in Heaven, I pray for the strength to always uphold truth in my speech and actions. In a world where falsehoods can easily entangle our lives, provide me with the courage to remain honest, even when it is difficult or costly. Let my words reflect Your truth, and my deeds demonstrate integrity, so that in all things, I might be a trustworthy servant and witness to Your teachings.

Guide me, Lord, to walk in truthfulness, fostering an environment where honesty is valued and upheld. Help me to influence others positively, encouraging them to embrace transparency and sincerity in their own lives. May my commitment to truth build stronger, more genuine relationships, and lead to just and honorable outcomes in every aspect of my service.

Amen.

# Prayer for the Environment

Lord, Creator of all, instill in us, your stewards, a deep respect and care for the environment as we conduct our duties. Grant us the wisdom to recognize the impact of our actions on nature and the foresight to implement practices that protect and preserve Your creation. Help us in the military to lead by example in environmental stewardship, ensuring that our operations and activities honor and sustain the natural world You have entrusted to us.

Inspire us to innovate and to find sustainable solutions that minimize harm to the earth while effectively fulfilling our mission. May our respect for the environment reflect our reverence for You, Lord, as we acknowledge our responsibility to care for the earth. Let us act with consideration not only for today's needs but also for the well-being of future generations, upholding our commitment to be caretakers of this planet.

Amen.

# Prayer for the Mentally Strained

Heavenly Father, I come to You burdened with the mental strains that weigh heavily upon me and my comrades. In the midst of pressures, stress, and the invisible wounds of service, grant us Your peace that surpasses all understanding. Heal our minds from anxiety, depression, and the many mental challenges that can arise from our duties. Provide us with strength and resilience, renewing our spirits and refreshing our thoughts.

Surround us with supportive relationships and resources that nurture mental well-being. Guide us to seek help when needed, and let us find solace in Your presence and Your promises. May we be reminded of Your constant care and the hope we have in You, which can illuminate even the darkest moments. Restore our mental clarity and stability, that we may serve with honor and live in joy.

Amen.

# Prayer for Faithfulness

Lord Almighty, imbue me with an unwavering faithfulness to our nation and the principles upon which it stands. As I serve, let my actions be guided by loyalty and a steadfast dedication to the well-being of our country and all its people. Help me to uphold the values of justice, liberty, and democracy, embodying these ideals in every aspect of my service. Strengthen my resolve to act with integrity and honor, representing our nation with pride and diligence.

Inspire in me, O God, a deep sense of commitment to my duties and to the fellow citizens I am sworn to protect. May I never waver in my responsibilities nor falter in my loyalties. Grant me the courage to make sacrifices required for the greater good, and the wisdom to see the paths that will best serve our country's future. Let my dedication be a reflection of Your divine faithfulness, guiding me to contribute positively and profoundly to our nation's legacy.

Amen.

# Prayer for the Coast Guard

Heavenly Father, I pray for the brave men and women of the Coast Guard who safeguard our waters. As they patrol the seas, perform rescues, and secure our borders, envelop them in Your protective care. Grant them wisdom and vigilance as they navigate challenging and often perilous conditions. Fortify their vessels and equipment, ensuring they are strong against the tumults of the ocean. May Your guiding hand be upon each member, steering them away from harm and toward successful completion of their missions.

Bless their efforts with clear communication, strong teamwork, and precise judgment. Provide calm seas and favorable weather, but when the storms arise, let their training and Your divine oversight see them through safely. Keep their spirits buoyant and their resolve unwavering as they fulfill their critical duties. May they feel Your presence with them on every voyage, returning safely to shore time and again.

Amen.

# Prayer for Personal Growth

Lord, I pray for personal growth and the development of virtues that reflect Your character. Instill in me the qualities of patience, kindness, humility, and strength. Help me to cultivate these traits through the daily challenges and interactions I face, that I might grow not only in competence but in character. May each experience refine me, removing impurities and building a stronger, more virtuous spirit within me.

Guide my thoughts and actions, Lord, so that I continuously seek improvement and strive toward the high calling You have placed on my life. Let my growth be evident to those around me, inspiring them to also pursue personal and spiritual development. In this journey of self-improvement, keep me grounded in Your word and steadfast in prayer, always reliant on Your grace and wisdom to transform me.

Amen.

# Prayer for Life Transitions

Heavenly Father, as I navigate the waters of change, whether transitioning from military to civilian life, moving to new locations, or embarking on new roles, grant me Your grace. These transitions, though often daunting, are part of Your plan for my growth and development. Help me to trust in Your timing and Your guidance, embracing each new chapter with courage and optimism. Provide me with the resilience to adapt and the wisdom to make decisions that align with Your will.

As I face these changes, surround me with supportive people who offer guidance and encouragement. Smooth the paths ahead and clear any obstacles in my way, making each transition not a time of stress but an opportunity for renewal and personal discovery. May Your peace reign in my heart through every adjustment and new beginning, keeping me steadfast in faith and purpose.

Amen.

# Prayer for Spiritual Renewal

Heavenly Father, I come before You seeking a renewal of my faith and spirit. In the weariness of life's battles and the routine of daily tasks, I sometimes feel my zeal dwindling and my passion cooling. Rekindle the fire within me, Lord. Refresh my soul with Your living waters and breathe new life into my walk with You. Ignite my heart with a renewed love for Your word and a deeper desire to engage in prayer and fellowship.

Strengthen my commitment to live out my faith actively, showing Your love through my actions and words. May this spiritual revival not only uplift my own spirit but also inspire those around me to seek You with renewed vigor. Let this renewal be evident in all aspects of my life, radiating Your light and love in clearer, more powerful ways. May my life testify to the transformative power of Your grace and the enduring hope found in You.

Amen.

# Prayer for Brotherhood

Heavenly Father, I pray for a spirit of brotherhood and unity among all who serve in our armed forces. Amidst the diversity of backgrounds, ranks, and roles, knit our hearts together in a bond of common purpose and mutual respect. Help us to support one another, to bear each other's burdens, and to celebrate each other's successes as if they were our own. May our relationships be marked by selflessness and a deep commitment to one another, reflecting the unity You desire for Your children.

Let this brotherhood extend beyond mere camaraderie to a profound connection that inspires trust, cooperation, and collective strength. In challenging times, may our solidarity be our fortress; in moments of triumph, our shared joy. Strengthen these bonds daily, that together we may face any adversity and accomplish great feats in Your name.

Amen.

# Prayer for Community Service

Lord, as I engage in community service, both in uniform and as a civilian, guide my efforts to have a meaningful impact on those I serve. Fill my heart with genuine compassion and an earnest desire to make a difference in my community. Grant me the creativity to identify the needs around me and the resourcefulness to address them effectively. Let my service be a testament to Your love and a beacon of hope to those in need.

Empower me to serve with humility and dedication, recognizing that every act of kindness, no matter how small, can significantly transform lives. Strengthen my resolve to contribute positively, fostering a spirit of community and mutual aid. May my actions inspire others to join in service, creating ripples of goodwill and change that resonate throughout our community and beyond. Amen.

# Prayer for Heritage and History

Heavenly Father, I give thanks for the rich heritage and enduring traditions of our military, which bind generations of servicemen and women together. Grant me, and all who serve, a deep respect for these traditions that shape our identity and guide our conduct. Help us to honor the legacy of those who came before us, appreciating their sacrifices and the path they paved for our freedom and security. Instill in us a sense of duty to uphold these values and pass them on, unblemished, to those who will follow.

As we carry forward this legacy, enlighten us to adapt wisely, blending respect for history with the insights of the present. May our reverence for military traditions inspire us to exemplary service and foster a continued commitment to excellence. Let us never forget the lessons of the past as we face the challenges of the future, ensuring that our actions today contribute honorably to the annals of our history.

Amen.

# Prayer for the Bereaved

Heavenly Father, my heart reaches out in prayer for all who have experienced the profound loss of a loved one, especially within our military community. In their grief and sorrow, be their comfort, their refuge, and their strength. Wrap Your loving arms around them, offering the peace that only You can provide. Help them to find solace in Your presence and the memories of those they have lost, knowing that Your love transcends the bounds of life and death.

Guide them through the dark valleys of mourning, and gently restore their spirits with hope and grace. May they feel connected to their loved ones through the bond of Your eternal care, and may they find community support that empathizes and aids in the healing process. Grant them moments of respite from their grief and the courage to face each new day with a sense of peace and renewed hope.

Amen.

# Prayer for Career Soldiers

Lord Almighty, I lift up those who have dedicated their lives to long-term service in our military. Strengthen their hearts and renew their spirits, that they may continue their service with unwavering perseverance and profound pride. Grant them the endurance needed to face the challenges that come with years of duty, and let their experience be a guiding light to the newer members of our armed forces. May they feel the weight of their achievements and the respect they have earned through their commitment and sacrifice.

Bless their path, O Lord, with continued purpose and opportunities for growth and leadership. Let their dedication inspire a sense of honor and duty in all of us who serve. Protect them, enrich their lives with joy and satisfaction, and provide them with the support of family, friends, and colleagues. May their legacy be one of courage, honor, and deep fulfillment, reflecting the best of our military traditions and values.

Amen.

# Prayer for Military Trainers

Heavenly Father, I pray for the dedicated military trainers who shape the future of our armed forces. Grant them wisdom to impart knowledge effectively and patience to guide their trainees through rigorous learning processes. May they find the right words and methods to inspire and educate, building not only skills but character in those they instruct. Help them to approach each day with enthusiasm and a commitment to excellence that motivates and transforms those under their guidance.

Bless their efforts, Lord, with clear outcomes and rewarding interactions. Sustain their energy and passion, preventing burnout and fostering a continuous love for teaching. Let them see the impact of their work in the success and growth of their trainees, reaffirming their vital role in maintaining the strength and readiness of our military. May their leadership and dedication echo through the lives of those they train, perpetuating a legacy of integrity and discipline.

Amen.

# Prayer for Ethical Decisions

Lord God, in moments of pressure and temptation, I seek Your guidance to uphold integrity and make ethical decisions. Fortify my resolve to act in accordance with Your will, ensuring that my choices reflect Your principles of truth and justice. Help me to remain steadfast in my commitment to righteousness, even when faced with difficult situations that test my moral compass. Provide me the courage to do what is right, not just what is easy or expedient, and to lead by example in all my endeavors.

Illuminate the path of virtue for me, that I may see clearly the way to proceed in honesty and honor. Let my decisions bring peace to my conscience and honor to Your name. Inspire those around me to also cherish and practice ethical behavior, creating an environment where integrity is the foundation of all actions. Through Your wisdom and strength, may I contribute to a legacy of ethical leadership and accountability in service to our nation.

Amen.

# Prayer for Military Intelligence

Heavenly Father, I pray for those who serve in military intelligence, that they may be endowed with accuracy in their analyses and discernment in their judgments. Equip them with the clarity and precision necessary to interpret information correctly and make informed decisions that will safeguard our nation and its people. Strengthen their commitment to truth and their ability to navigate the complexities of data they encounter, ensuring their work leads to secure and beneficial outcomes.

Grant them wisdom to foresee potential challenges and opportunities, allowing them to act proactively rather than reactively. Protect them from the pitfalls of misinformation and guide them in their efforts to provide reliable and timely intelligence. May their work be guided by Your hand, ensuring that they serve with integrity and contribute positively to our national security. Let their discernment reflect Your higher wisdom, bringing light to dark places and clarity to shadows.

Amen.

# Prayer for Victory

Heavenly Father, I come before You seeking Your favor and guidance for victory in our endeavors and conflicts. May our efforts, whether in peaceful pursuits or in the defense of our nation, be crowned with success that glorifies Your name. Grant us wisdom to navigate challenges effectively and the strength to overcome obstacles. In moments of conflict, guide our decisions and actions so that we may achieve outcomes that ensure safety, promote peace, and uphold justice.

Surround us with Your protection and lead us through each battle with Your right hand uplifted in our favor. Help us to remember that true victory comes through righteousness and that success is measured not only in achievements but in the integrity of our actions. May our victories reflect Your divine providence and bring about greater good for our nation and the world. Instill in us a spirit of gratitude for every triumph, attributing each success to Your gracious empowerment.

Amen.

# Prayer for Reintegration

Heavenly Father, as I transition from military to civilian life, I seek Your guidance and comfort in this period of change. Help me to reintegrate smoothly into a daily routine that no longer includes the regimented structure I am accustomed to. Provide me with the patience and wisdom to adjust to new environments and relationships, and to find my place in a community that may seem as unfamiliar as it is familiar.

Bless me with opportunities that leverage my skills and experiences from service, allowing me to continue contributing meaningfully to society. Ease the emotional and psychological challenges that come with this transition, and surround me with supportive people who understand and encourage my journey back to civilian life. May Your peace fill my heart and Your strength guide my steps as I navigate this new chapter, finding fulfillment and purpose anew.

Amen.

# Prayer for Personal Courage

Lord, I come to You in need of courage, not just the bravery that is seen on the battlefield, but the courage to face the personal battles that challenge me daily. Help me confront my fears, insecurities, and the struggles within that no one else may see. Infuse my spirit with Your strength, so I may stand resilient and move forward with confidence, knowing You are with me every step of the way.

Guide me to overcome these inner conflicts with grace and determination, allowing me to grow and emerge stronger. Let Your wisdom lead my decisions, Your patience calm my spirit, and Your love encourage my heart. In moments of doubt and hesitation, remind me of Your unending support and the victories I have already achieved through Your guidance. May this personal courage not only enhance my life but also inspire those around me to confront their challenges with the same boldness.

Amen.

# Prayer for the Oath of Enlistment

Heavenly Father, as I take the Oath of Enlistment, imbue me with a deep sense of reverence and commitment to the duties I am about to assume. Let this moment be a solemn affirmation of my dedication to serve our nation with honor, courage, and integrity. Help me to fully grasp the weight of the responsibilities laid upon my shoulders, inspiring me to uphold them faithfully throughout my service.

May this oath not merely be words I recite, but a powerful declaration of my commitment to defend and protect. Strengthen my resolve to adhere to this promise, guiding me in my actions and decisions, so that I may contribute positively and uphold the values and ideals of our military and country. Let this commitment extend beyond the uniform, influencing every aspect of my life, and reinforcing my dedication to service and excellence.

Amen.

# Prayer for Military Anniversaries

Heavenly Father, as we mark another military anniversary, I am filled with gratitude for the years of service and the milestones achieved. Let this time of reflection bring to mind the sacrifices made and the victories won, strengthening our bonds and renewing our commitment to our mission. Help us to celebrate these moments not just as memories of the past, but as inspirations for our continued service and dedication.

During this anniversary, rekindle in us a spirit of pride and gratitude for all that has been accomplished, and a renewed vision for the future. May we honor those who have served before us and those who serve alongside us, recognizing the collective effort that has sustained our force. Let this celebration be a reminder of Your constant guidance and support, and a reaffirmation of our pledge to serve with honor, courage, and integrity.

Amen.

# Prayer for Tactical Skill

Lord of Wisdom, as I engage in operations that require precision and strategic insight, I seek Your guidance to enhance my tactical skills. Grant me the proficiency to execute my duties effectively, making wise decisions that lead to successful outcomes. Equip me with a clear mind and a keen understanding of tactics, that I may anticipate challenges and maneuver through them with expertise.

Inspire me and my team with innovative strategies and the ability to adapt quickly to changing circumstances. Strengthen our collaboration and communication, ensuring that each move is coordinated and effective, reflecting careful planning and Your divine inspiration. May our efforts be marked by excellence and lead to the safety and success of all involved.

Amen.

# Prayer for Endurance

Heavenly Father, as I face the demand of long operations and enduring challenges, I seek Your sustaining power to fortify my stamina and resolve. Help me to persevere through fatigue and difficulty, keeping my spirit vigilant and my body strong. Infuse me with Your enduring strength that does not falter, even when the end seems distant and the task arduous. May Your grace uplift me, preventing weariness from diminishing my capacity to serve effectively.

Encourage my heart, Lord, when the hours stretch long and the workload increases. Renew my energy and focus, allowing me to maintain the pace and quality of my efforts. Let Your presence be a constant source of comfort and motivation, reminding me that with You, all things are sustained and all challenges can be met. Grant me the resilience to continue, pushing forward until the mission is accomplished, with my faith and duty steadfastly intact.

Amen.

# Prayer for the National Guard

Heavenly Father, I pray for the men and women of the National Guard, who stand ready to respond at a moment's notice, whether to natural disasters, crises, or national needs. Bless them with vigilance, readiness, and the strength to face each challenge with courage and efficiency. Guide their leaders, grant them wisdom in decision-making, and ensure their strategies and efforts are effective and safe.

Equip each member of the National Guard with the skills and resources needed to perform their duties successfully. Protect them as they protect us, fortifying their resolve and resilience. May they feel supported by their communities and strengthened by Your presence, knowing they do not stand alone. Inspire them with a spirit of service and a commitment to excellence in all their responses.

Amen.

# Prayer for Moral Challenges

Lord, in the face of moral challenges and ethical dilemmas, I seek Your guidance to act with virtue and integrity. Illuminate my path with Your wisdom, enabling me to discern right from wrong in complex situations where the answers are not clear. Grant me the clarity to understand the implications of my choices, and the courage to choose the path that aligns with Your principles and honors my commitment to serve justly.

Strengthen my resolve to uphold ethical standards, even when faced with pressures that tempt me to compromise. Let Your truth be my guide, and Your love my motivation, as I navigate these trials. Help me to embody the values I stand for, acting as a beacon of righteousness for those I lead and serve alongside. In all things, may my actions reflect Your moral perfection and bring glory to Your name.

Amen.

# Prayer for Overseas Service

Heavenly Father, as I serve overseas, far from home and familiar comforts, grant me strength and ensure my safety under Your watchful eye. Surround me with Your protection as I navigate new environments and face the uncertainties that come with foreign lands. Infuse me with courage and resilience, that I may fulfill my duties with honor and effectiveness, serving as a testament to the values we uphold.

Keep my spirit uplifted amidst the challenges and loneliness that may come, reminding me of the support and prayers from home that follow me. Provide wisdom to my commanders and unity among my peers, ensuring that together, we achieve our objectives while maintaining our moral compass. May Your presence be a constant comfort, guiding every step and decision I make while serving abroad.

Amen.

# Prayer for Strategic Minds

Lord Almighty, bless me with a strategic mind, endowed with the foresight and acumen necessary for effective planning and decision-making. As I undertake responsibilities that require deep insight and careful thought, guide my thoughts to be clear and my judgments sound. Help me to foresee potential outcomes and prepare accordingly, that my actions may not only respond to present challenges but also pave the way for future successes.

Grant me the wisdom to collaborate effectively with others, to draw upon collective experiences and knowledge, enhancing our ability to strategize with precision. May my plans align with Your greater purpose and contribute to the well-being and safety of those I serve alongside. Strengthen my resolve to face complex situations with confidence, trusting in Your guidance to navigate every decision.

Amen.

# Prayer for Camaraderie

Heavenly Father, I pray for the deepening of camaraderie among my colleagues and me as we serve together. Strengthen the bonds of friendship and support that unite us, enabling us to face the myriad challenges of our duties with a united front. Instill in us a spirit of brotherhood and sisterhood that transcends the ordinary, fostering relationships built on trust, respect, and mutual understanding.

Help us to lean on one another in times of need and to celebrate together in times of joy. May our connections be a source of strength and comfort, enhancing our effectiveness and morale. Encourage us to always extend a helping hand and a listening ear, ensuring no one feels isolated or unsupported. Through this fellowship, may we not only succeed in our missions but also grow personally and collectively, reflecting Your love in our unity.

Amen.

# Prayer for Honorable Discharge

Lord, as I approach the conclusion of my military service and prepare for honorable discharge, I offer You my deepest gratitude for guiding me through every step of this journey. Thank You for the strength, courage, and perseverance You bestowed upon me, allowing me to serve my country with honor and dignity. As this chapter closes, I reflect on the experiences that have shaped me and the lessons learned, grateful for both the challenges and the triumphs.

Bless this transition, O God, and fill my heart with hope and excitement for the future. May the skills and values I have gained during my service continue to influence my life positively and inspire others. Recognize, Lord, the contributions of all who complete their service, granting them peace and fulfillment in their new endeavors. Let us carry forward the pride of our accomplishments, confident in the foundation we have built for continued growth and service in different capacities.

Amen.

# Prayer for Service Anniversaries

Heavenly Father, today I pause to acknowledge and celebrate my service anniversary, reflecting on the journey that has brought me to this milestone. I am filled with gratitude for the strength You have provided, the wisdom You have imparted, and the guidance You have offered throughout my service. This anniversary not only marks a passage of time but symbolizes the growth, challenges overcome, and the contributions I have made in the line of duty.

As I commemorate this special day, I ask for Your continued blessings in the years to come. May this milestone serve as a reminder of the purpose and passion that drive my commitment to serve. Inspire me to pursue excellence continually, to learn from each experience, and to lead with integrity and honor. Let this anniversary renew my dedication and enthusiasm for the responsibilities and opportunities that lie ahead.

Amen.

# Prayer for Deployment Preparation

Heavenly Father, as I prepare for deployment, I seek Your guidance and strength to equip me both physically and spiritually. Let Your wisdom lead my preparations, ensuring that I am ready to face the tasks and challenges ahead. Instill in me a sense of peace and resolve, removing any anxiety or fear, and replacing it with confidence and trust in Your protection.

Surround me with Your presence, Lord, and reinforce my spirit with Your courage as I step into new responsibilities. Bless my family and loved ones with peace of mind, knowing that Your loving arms encircle them just as they do me. Prepare my heart and mind for the journey ahead, ensuring that I carry Your assurance and calm into every situation I will encounter.

Amen.

# Prayer for Non-Commissioned Officers

Heavenly Father, I lift up all non-commissioned officers who bear the weight of leadership and responsibility within their ranks. Grant them the wisdom to guide those under their command with integrity and strength. Fill their hearts with the courage to enforce discipline gently and the insight to lead by example, fostering an environment of respect and cooperation. May their leadership reflect Your justice and mercy, encouraging each member to strive for excellence and unity.

Strengthen their resolve when they face the pressures of their duties, and grant them patience in challenges and decision-making. Help them to balance authority with compassion, ensuring their actions and words nurture the potential of those they lead. May their influence inspire their teams to greater achievements and deeper commitment to their service. Bless them with a continuous growth in leadership skills and personal character, that they may serve well in every task entrusted to them.

Amen.

# Prayer for Military Engineers

Heavenly Father, I pray for the military engineers who apply their skills in service to our nation. Grant them ingenuity and creativity as they design and construct solutions that support our missions and safeguard lives. Bestow upon them precision and excellence in their work, ensuring that each project they undertake is robust and effective, reflecting the critical nature of their tasks. May their minds be sharp and their solutions innovative, pushing the boundaries of technology and strategy for superior outcomes.

Protect these skilled men and women as they operate in both safe environments and zones of conflict. Provide them safety as they face the physical dangers associated with their duties, and guide their hands to prevent accidents and ensure successful completions of their projects. May they work with confidence, knowing that their efforts are shielded by Your watchful care and guided by Your wisdom.

Amen.

# Prayer for Historical Battles

Lord God, as I reflect upon the historical battles that have shaped our nation and our military, I am grateful for the lessons they have taught us. Help us to honor the courage and sacrifices of those who fought, by learning from their experiences and applying these lessons to better ourselves and our methods. May the history of conflict not only remind us of the costs of war but also inspire us to pursue peace and strategic wisdom.

Guide us in our study and remembrance of these pivotal moments, ensuring that we do not forget the past but use it to inform our present and future actions. Let the bravery and endurance exhibited in these battles strengthen our resolve to serve with honor and integrity. May we also seek reconciliation where there has been strife, fostering a spirit of unity and mutual respect both within our ranks and with our global neighbors.

Amen.

# Prayer for Military Justice

Heavenly Father, I pray for the principle of justice to reign within our military system, ensuring fairness and lawfulness in all our proceedings. Guide the hands and hearts of those who administer military justice, from the judges to the juries and the attorneys. Infuse their work with Your wisdom and integrity, that they might render decisions that are just and true. Protect them from partiality and corruption, and instill in them a deep respect for the law and the rights of all individuals under their jurisdiction.

Let our military justice system be a model of righteousness and ethical conduct, reflecting the values we stand to defend. May every case handled be approached with diligence and the pursuit of truth, ensuring that justice is not only served but upheld with the highest standards. Strengthen our commitment to maintaining a discipline that is fair and a system that respects the dignity of each person, fostering trust and honor among all service members.

Amen.

# Prayer for the Silent Ranks

Heavenly Father, I lift up in prayer those who serve in the silent ranks, the many men and women in support roles who are the backbone of our military operations. Though often unseen and unrecognized, their contributions are vital to our success. Grant them a sense of pride and accomplishment in their work, knowing that every task they perform is essential to the greater mission. Strengthen their spirits and encourage their hearts, that they may feel valued and integral to our collective efforts.

Bless them with patience and perseverance as they fulfill their duties. May they be equipped with the resources they need to perform effectively and receive the support necessary to thrive in their positions. Instill in all of us a deep appreciation for their work, fostering an environment of mutual respect and gratitude across all levels of service. Let us never underestimate the power of the support given, and may we always acknowledge the critical impact of these silent ranks.

Amen.

# Prayer for Civilian-Military Relations

Heavenly Father, I pray for the strengthening of relations between our military personnel and the civilian communities they serve and protect. Foster a spirit of mutual respect and understanding between us, that both civilians and service members may appreciate each other's roles and contributions to our nation's security and well-being. Remove any barriers of misunderstanding or mistrust, replacing them with cooperation and a shared commitment to upholding the common good.

Encourage dialogue and engagement that bridges gaps and builds bonds of friendship and collaboration. Inspire leaders on both sides to initiate and support activities that increase interaction and enhance mutual appreciation. May our actions reflect Your love and promote peace, so that together, as one community united under God, we can face the challenges and celebrate the triumphs that affect our country.

Amen.

# Prayer for Healing Divisions

Heavenly Father, in a world where divisions often arise, I ask for Your healing touch to mend the fractures within our military forces and foster unity amidst our diversity. Help us to see the strength that comes from our differences, turning them into opportunities for learning and growth rather than sources of separation. Instill in each of us a spirit of brotherhood and sisterhood, respecting and valuing each unique background, belief, and perspective that enriches our collective experience.

Guide our leaders and all service members in building bridges of understanding and cooperation. May our actions and interactions reflect Your teachings of love and acceptance, promoting a culture of inclusivity. Let our unity be a beacon of hope and a testament to the power of Your love, proving that together, we are stronger and more effective in fulfilling our mission and duties.

Amen.

# Prayer for Psychological Health

Heavenly Father, I come before You seeking Your support for the psychological health and wellness of myself and my fellow service members. Amidst the pressures and challenges we face daily, grant us mental strength and resilience. Protect our minds from the stress and trauma that can accompany our duties, and provide pathways for healing and recovery when we are wounded in spirit. Nurture our mental well-being with Your peace, ensuring we have access to the resources and support necessary to maintain our psychological health.

Guide those who provide care—psychologists, counselors, and chaplains—in their work to help us find balance and strength. May they be equipped with wisdom and compassion to effectively aid those in need. Help us to recognize the signs of mental strain in ourselves and others, encouraging a culture where seeking help is honored, not stigmatized. Renew our spirits daily, Lord, so that we may continue to serve with vigor and virtue, embodying the fullness of health that You intend for each of us.

Amen.

# Prayer for Physical Training

Lord, as I engage in physical training and strive to maintain my health and fitness, grant me the endurance and strength necessary to meet and exceed the demands placed upon my body. Help me to persevere through the rigors of training, finding joy in the challenge and improvement of my physical abilities. May my efforts in fitness serve not only to enhance my performance but also to fortify my overall well-being, enabling me to fulfill my duties with energy and vigor.

Bless my body with resilience to injuries and quick recovery when they occur. Instill in me a discipline that extends beyond routine workouts, influencing my choices in nutrition, rest, and self-care. Let my physical training be a reflection of my dedication to service, preparing me fully for the tasks at hand. Through this discipline, may I glorify You with my body, keeping it a strong and capable vessel for the work You have set before me.

Amen.

# Prayer for Devine Leadership

Heavenly Father, as I take on roles of leadership and command, I earnestly seek Your divine guidance to steer my decisions and actions. Illuminate my path with Your wisdom, that I may lead with justice, integrity, and compassion. Help me to embody the qualities of a godly leader—humility, strength, and discernment—so that I can effectively guide those under my command towards our shared goals while nurturing their growth and well-being.

Grant me the foresight to anticipate challenges and the clarity to navigate them wisely. In moments of uncertainty, remind me to turn to You for the answers, trusting that You will lead me through every difficulty. Let my leadership reflect Your love and serve as a testament to Your sovereign rule over all. May those I lead see Your light in me, inspiring them to also seek Your guidance in their lives.

Amen.

# Prayer for the Marine Corps

Heavenly Father, I lift up the brave men and women of the Marine Corps, who uphold the proud traditions and valorous spirit of their service. Strengthen them, Lord, with courage and resolve as they face the rigorous demands and dangers of their duties. Infuse their hearts with steadfast bravery and a commitment to excellence that honors the rich heritage of the Marine Corps. May they continue to exemplify the core values of honor, courage, and commitment in every task and challenge.

Bless them with your protection as they stand at the forefront of our nation's defense. Guide their leaders with wisdom and foresight, ensuring that the traditions of the past seamlessly blend with the innovations of the present to forge a stronger future. May the Marine Corps remain a symbol of resilience and dedication, inspiring all who look upon them with a deep respect for their service and sacrifices.

Amen.

# Prayer for Special Operations Forces

Heavenly Father, I call upon Your guidance and protection for the men and women serving in our Special Operations Forces. As they undertake missions that demand the utmost stealth and precision, cloak them in Your divine protection, allowing them to move undetected and act effectively under the cover of Your grace. Sharpen their skills and their senses, that they may execute their tasks with flawless accuracy and return safely from each operation.

Grant them the mental clarity and physical agility required for their demanding roles. Strengthen their resolve and fortify their courage as they face the unknown, equipping them with calm under pressure and decisiveness in the face of danger. May their efforts contribute to peace and security, and may they feel Your presence continuously guiding and watching over them in every challenging endeavor.

Amen.

# Afterword

As we reach the conclusion of this collection, it is my hope that these prayers have resonated with those who serve, those who have served, and the families that support them. The journey of a military member is marked by unique challenges and profound experiences—moments of valor, sacrifice, and often, great personal cost. These prayers are intended to offer solace, guidance, and strength to navigate the often turbulent waters of military life.

May these prayers be a source of comfort and encouragement, reminding you of the divine presence that accompanies each soldier, sailor, airman, marine, and coast guardsman. Let them serve not only as petitions but also as reminders of the support and gratitude that your service inspires in the hearts of your fellow citizens.

As you turn the pages of this book, whether in moments of quiet reflection or urgent need, may you find the words that speak to your situation and uplift your spirit. Above all, may you feel connected—both to the divine and to the vast community of those who share the bond of service.

God bless you, your service, and your journey, wherever it may lead.

Carter Birmingham

Made in United States
Troutdale, OR
09/29/2024

23243289R00058